Original title:
Tassels and Whispers

Copyright © 2025 Creative Arts Management OÜ
All rights reserved.

Author: Elliot Harrison
ISBN HARDBACK: 978-1-80586-003-7
ISBN PAPERBACK: 978-1-80586-475-2

Lurking in the Fringe

In the corner, something shakes,
A fuzzy thing with funny fakes.
It giggles and it jives around,
What secrets lie beneath that sound?

With every sway, a curious peek,
Dancing shadows that dare to speak.
A flicker here, then gone from view,
What mischief lurks, we're not sure who!

The Subtle Touch of Silence

Silent giggles in the air,
An echo hiding everywhere.
A nod, a wink, a quiet cheer,
What's that lurking, oh so near?

The air is thick with quiet fun,
A toe-tap here, a little run.
With whispers bright, they plot and plan,
Invisible tricks, oh how they can!

Threads of Enigma

A knot of tales that twist and twine,
With every pull, the stories shine.
A jumbled mess, yet somehow clear,
In every loop, there's grinning cheer.

Threads that dance with life and zest,
Each a riddle, a playful jest.
Untangle me, if you dare,
Giggles scatter everywhere!

Whispers Beneath the Surface

Underneath, the giggles slide,
A playful breeze, a secret ride.
They bubble up, with zest and charm,
Hiding there, away from harm.

The ground does rumble, a chuckle here,
Tickles of humor, never sheer.
What mysteries lie below our feet?
In every stomp, a laugh to greet!

Veils of Unspoken Thoughts

In a corner, secrets play,
Tickling ears in a sly ballet.
Giggling shadows, they conspire,
Leaving laughter like a choir.

Chatting hats on heads askew,
Unraveled tales, a motley crew.
With every glance, a wink, a jest,
In silent jokes, they find their rest.

The Dance of Fading Hues

Colors twirl in a silly spree,
Dancing lightly, oh so free.
Pinks and greens poke fun at blue,
Laughing 'til their faces hue.

Swirls of orange tease the crowd,
While giggles rise, both soft and loud.
They slip and slide without a care,
Brightly blowing through the air.

Sheen of Secrets in Dusk

At twilight, chuckles loom above,
Whispers of folly, full of love.
Sparkling stories drift and glide,
With each tease, the stars collide.

Glimmers twinkling like a grin,
Echoes hinting where they've been.
In the dusk, the jesters play,
Imaginary frays lead astray.

Silhouettes in Threaded Air

Shadows dance with silly grace,
Skipping lightly in a race.
Frayed edges giggle, stretch and sway,
In the midst of a twilight fray.

A wink of light and then a blur,
Frolicking whispers start to stir.
With each movement, jokes appear,
Tickling laughter, loud and clear.

Solar Threads of Affection

In sunlight's glow, we play and tease,
A dance of colors, fluttering with ease.
Stitch by stitch, we laugh and twirl,
Embroidery dreams in a vibrant swirl.

With every knot, a chuckle grows,
Tickling each other, oh how it flows!
Laughter woven into every seam,
Haphazard joys, more silly than a dream.

The Sweetness of Illustration

Doodles circle round our heads,
Like candy clouds on sleepy beds.
The sketches giggle, jump and play,
Ticklish lines in a bright ballet.

Colors run like wild confetti,
As giggles spill, oh isn't it petty!
With every stroke, a grin appears,
Painted mischief to chase the fears.

Folded Dreams in Gentle Embrace

Origami hearts, in silly glee,
Flap their corners, so unpredictably.
They tease the wind with little flings,
Like paper birds on dainty wings.

A fold here, a crease right there,
We burst with laughter—who would dare?
Each masterpiece, a giggling prank,
In our craft club, we live in a prank.

Murmurs in Twisted Fiber

Woolly whispers churn and spin,
With every twist, the fun begins.
Knots and purls in joyful chat,
Crafting giggles where we're at.

The yarn confides with playful yarn,
Spinning tales of joy and charm.
As stitches clack, our giggles roar,
We stitch our secrets forevermore.

Touches of a Fading Light

In the corner, shadows dance,
A sock puppet takes a chance.
With wiggly arms and silly grin,
It tells the tales where laughter spins.

A fading glow, oh what a sight,
When dinner plans take off at night.
Some noodles fly, a fork does glide,
In this kitchen, chaos can't hide.

Secrets Between the Lines

A book reads me like I read it,
Caught in a plot, I quietly sit.
Turns out a cat wrote every scene,
A tale of fish and a whacky queen.

Each page a giggle, a chuckle here,
Characters whisper, 'No one can hear!'
Between each line, a sneaky wink,
In this book world, we all just think.

Luminescence of Subtlety

Glow sticks beckon at the fair,
A dance party starts without a care.
Silly moves and brighter hues,
As air balloons float like a ruse.

The night wears laughter, sweet and light,
Balloons collide, what a funny sight!
Even the stars twinkle with glee,
At this carnival, wild and free.

Weaving the Language of Dreams

In dreams, a llama speaks in rhyme,
Wearing a sweater, looking sublime.
He shares his thoughts on pizza pies,
And how to score the perfect fries.

A tapestry of thoughts so bright,
With unicorns dancing in moonlight.
Each thread a giggle, a twist of fate,
In dreamland's realm, all is first-rate.

Tender Touch of the Unheard

A cat in a hat, so sly and spry,
Winks at the dog, who just wonders why.
They dance in the moonlight, quite a sight,
Chasing each other, oh what a delight!

The parrot drops pearls, with a squawk and a flip,
While the goldfish snickers, hiding in a dip.
Together they plot, a party in case,
With a banana as crown, in this quirky place.

Where Dreams Intertwine.

In a teacup castle, they sip and they chat,
With a muffin for a throne, and a cookie for a mat.
They play chess with jellybeans, sweet and round,
While the gnome on the shelf keeps spinning around.

A frog in a tux, does a little jig,
While the owl wears glasses, looking quite big.
They laugh at the moon's funny little frown,
As the sun takes a nap, rolling over to brown.

Fringed Dreams of Silence

There's a snail in the garden, racing a bee,
With a leaf as a finish, as funny as can be.
They chuckle at daisies, who sway with the breeze,
While the worms in the dirt play hopscotch with ease.

A mouse in a shoe, with a dance so grand,
Trying on socks, that he can hardly stand.
With every wrong step, the tune gets more bright,
In this silly affair, everything feels right.

Murmurs in the Shadows

A shadowy corner, where giggles reside,
With a hedgehog in sneakers, who runs with pride.
He bumps into hedges, giggling with glee,
As the dandelions cheer, that's the place to be!

A raccoon in glasses, counting the stars,
While a fox plays the lute, sits softly on Mars.
They ponder the cosmos, and joke about fate,
In this crowded dreamland, nothing's too late.

Threads of Hope Intertwined

In a world of yarn and cheer,
The stitches dance, my dear.
Each color tells a tale,
Of mishaps that never fail.

A button's lost, a seam unsewn,
Fabric speaks where words have flown.
Laughter echoes, needle pricks,
What a mix of crafty tricks!

Patterns clash in vibrant play,
Socks that no one dares to sway.
The quilt sings of joy and plight,
Stitch it up, it feels just right!

When friends gather with thread in hand,
Giggles form the perfect band.
Knots undone with playful grace,
In this tangled, cozy space.

Whispers Captured in Fabric

A patchwork quilt with stories spun,
Each piece a secret, just for fun.
Thread the needle, hear them laugh,
Best friends share their goofy gaffs.

A tassel here, a fringe askew,
What's this project? No one knew!
Oops, a snag, oh what a sight,
Let's claim it's modern art tonight!

Fabrics clash, a perfect mess,
Who knew sewing could impress?
With silken threads and laughter loud,
We wear our quirks, we're so proud!

As patterns twist and tales unfold,
A fabric bond we've made, behold!
In cozy corners, we'll find our cheer,
Crafting memories, year by year.

Soft Caresses on Fabricated Hearts

A feathered tickle on the cheek,
Sparks of laughter, joy we seek.
Threads of humor stitched with care,
Poking fun, we're light as air.

Pillow fights and silly pranks,
With every fold, we share our ranks.
Laughter stitched in every seam,
Fabric hearts, we're one big dream.

Silenced Journeys in Stitches

Wobbly seams avoid the fuss,
Lost in stitches, what's the rush?
A sock that danced upon the floor,
Now we giggle, wanting more.

Bobbins spinning tales so bright,
In the twilight, full of light.
Silent travels, oh, what fun,
In our laughter, we have won.

Intimate Whispers of the Heart

Secret chuckles tucked away,
In every stitch, a game we play.
A button's wink, a zipper's hush,
In quiet giggles, we all blush.

Velvet tales of joy unwind,
Crafting moments, sweetly blind.
With every wave of fabric's bend,
We find humor, life's best friend.

A Symphony of Hidden Texture

With a crinkle here and rustle there,
A melody of moments shared.
Tickles hidden in each fold,
Stories wrapped in threads of gold.

A ruffled charm, a playful flare,
Whimsical tunes float in the air.
Every texture, a tale appears,
In every laugh, we shed our fears.

Gossamer Echoes of Memory

In the attic, secrets play,
Dust bunnies dance, bright and gay.
Old hats tip with a jaunty air,
While the cat surveys with a lazy stare.

Once a sock had so much flair,
Now it's lost, it's beyond repair.
The giggles of yarn, a ladder of fun,
Unraveling tales, one by one.

Stray buttons wink with mischievous glee,
Each a story, a puzzle's decree.
From tangled threads, laughter sprouts,
Echoes of yarn trips, oh the shouts!

Memories wrapped in a patchwork quilt,
Knots of joy and chaos built.
With every wink, the past takes a bow,
Reminding us to chuckle here and now.

Whispers from Woven Corners

In a corner, threads collide,
They giggle softly, can't hide their pride.
The fabric folds like a teasing grin,
As hidden stitches let the fun begin.

A tale untold, of a wayward seam,
That turned a shirt into quite the meme.
Patterns twirl in a whimsical dance,
Playing hide-and-seek without a chance.

Buttons laugh, and zippers play,
Hitching a ride on a sunny day.
Fabric scraps in a joyful race,
Fleeing from needles, oh, what a chase!

In woven corners, joy takes shape,
Twisted threads weave a silly cape.
As laughter stitches across the room,
These playful whispers banish gloom.

Hidden Voices of the Loom

In the clatter of a busy room,
Threads whisper tales of yarn and gloom.
Looms chuckle, bobbins spin,
As they weave out secrets, eager to begin.

Each thread a joker, each knot a prank,
The warp and weft dance in a happy flank.
A spool of laughter rolls off the shelf,
With each twist, they make quite the elf.

Loom's deep belly, a treasure chest,
Hiding giggles, never at rest.
Patterns like riddles, unraveled and spun,
As hidden voices sing just for fun.

From the weaver's hands, a stitchy jest,
Creating chaos—oh, who would have guessed?
With each gentle tug, hilarity ensues,
In the fabric of life, we blend our hues.

The Caress of Hanging Hues

Beneath the line where colors swing,
Swaying curtains make the room sing.
They tease the light, a playful sweep,
In cheer-drenched shades, giggles leap.

In each flutter, whispers flare,
As playful hues dance through the air.
A polka dot called out a plaid,
Together, they made quirky and mad.

The tapestry giggles, a riotous green,
Mixing and mashing, quite the scene.
With each blend comes a hearty cheer,
As colors conspire, our laughter draws near.

So let them sway, let them tease,
Hanging hues that aim to please.
In rooms of color, delight will bloom,
Creating a carnival—life's joyful room.

Fragile Links of Human Touch

In a dance of threads we twirl,
Caught in loops, what a swirl!
With each tug, giggles arise,
Crafting chaos in disguise.

Laughter stitches every seam,
Life's a comic little dream.
We're all tangled, making fret,
In this fabric of duet.

A tug and pull, what's the fuss?
Who knew yarn could cause such rust?
With silly knots and jests we share,
Friendship's fabric, light as air.

As we knit our lives together,
Choose bright colors, light as feather.
With every stitch a new delight,
Oh, what fun in threads of light!

Silent Revelations in Knitted Dreams

In cozy corners we convene,
With balls of yarn, the moments green.
A slip, a stitch, oh what a tale,
As we laugh and sip hot ale.

Purling secrets, hushed and bright,
As needles click through day and night.
Each loop reveals a funny side,
With each mistake, we laugh and bide.

Revelations in our craft abound,
As tangled hues spin round and round.
The truth comes out in shades of glee,
In knitted warmth, we're wild and free.

Silent giggles in the weave,
Though frayed and odd, just don't deceive.
For in each knot lies joy's embrace,
A comical twist in this warm place.

Embroidered Fate

Stitches weaving silly signs,
In our fate, a jumbled line.
Every thread, a twist of fate,
Laughing at what we create.

With colors bold, we seldom miss,
Crafting joy in every stitch.
A knot here, a loop there, so bright,
Who knew fate could be such a delight?

Dancing threads like ants on a spree,
Embroidered laughs, oh so free.
With tangled tales we birth with care,
In every snip, a giggling flair.

Our fortunes spelled in bright arrays,
What a sight, life's funny ways.
Each design tells a tale anew,
In stitches bold, we see it through!

Shadows in Finely Woven Silence

In quiet corners, shadows play,
Woven whispers lead astray.
With every thread, a secret laugh,
As we chart out our own path.

In silence, tangled stories bloom,
A merry chaos fills the room.
Life's mishaps sewn in jest,
Each knot a giggle, not a rest.

Fiction spun in every hue,
Threads of laughter tint the view.
We dance in shadows of our thread,
Whimsical dreams in laughter spread.

In secret seams, jokes reside,
With every twist, we giggle wide.
What a tangled life we face,
In woven silence, find our grace!

Fringed Secrets

In corners where the giggles dwell,
A secret stash of tales to tell.
With every loop and every curl,
The fabric dances, making us twirl.

Beneath the bright, rainbow hues,
Laughter hides in playful clues.
Each snip and stitch, a joke in hand,
Creating chaos, oh so grand!

When threads entwine like friends at play,
They tease and tickle in a funny way.
A poking stitch, a little tug,
In the fabric world, we all snug!

So take a peek, join in the fun,
Where frayed ends gleam under the sun.
A patchwork quilt of quirks and sight,
In this whimsical fabric, all feels right!

Hushed Threads

In quiet rooms, the stories creep,
Softly shared, not loud nor deep.
A stitch unravels the quiet night,
With every hem, the giggles ignite.

In secret seams, the whispers squeak,
A fabric joke, no need to peak.
Binding tales with little sighs,
They weave through time with twinkling eyes.

When things go wrong, how patterns twist,
The kind of fun you can't resist.
Knots that tangle, a fabric brawl,
A patchwork of laughter, we'll embrace it all!

Each quiet thread, a sneaky jest,
In the world of fabric, we are blessed.
So here we sit, with threads in hand,
Stitching laughter across the land!

The Dance of Delicate Fragments

A flurry of bits, a thumping beat,
They twirl and swirl, oh what a treat!
Fragmented dreams in a vibrant dance,
Hopping around, giving chance a chance.

With snippets here and patches there,
They laugh and sing without a care.
Jumps and spins, like craftsmen chums,
Creating joy where silliness hums.

These fragments of life, a funny show,
They whisper secrets only we know.
With every stitch, a giggle stitched tight,
In this fabric world, we take flight!

So hold your seams, and let them sway,
Dance with us in this bright display.
For in every twirl, there's fun to find,
A piece of laughter, forever entwined!

Soft Echoes of Elegance

Elegant whispers, plush and light,
Soft echoes bounce, taking flight.
In folds and creases, laughter hides,
Among the fabrics where fun resides.

A playful twirl, a graceful tease,
With every riffle, we giggle with ease.
Fanciful patterns, a comical fable,
Turning the mundane into a table.

The elegance plays, a humorous guise,
Each gentle fold, a laugh in disguise.
With charming flair, they waltz around,
In the serene silence, joy is found!

So let's embrace this playful cheer,
In delicate spaces, we draw near.
With echoes soft and tales galore,
In this fabric garden, we explore!

Frayed Edges of Memory

In the attic, dust bunnies play,
Old socks dance, in their own ballet.
Grandma's tales, a bit out of tune,
Spinning yarns beneath a lightened moon.

A cat naps, dreaming of tuna and cheese,
While a lost hat flits with the autumn breeze.
Photos faded, colors gone bold,
Stories retold, never get old.

Boys in the garden, flying a plane,
Their giggles a melody, sweet but insane.
A chicken struts like a feathered king,
Clucking a tune, can you hear it sing?

Frames of memories, a collage of fun,
Worn out laughter, like a well-loved run.
With every border torn just a bit,
Life moments, crazy, never quite fit.

Veils of Serenity

A cloth hangs limply, a stage for a show,
Where dust motes dance as the soft winds blow.
A squirrel scampers, with a nut in tow,
While the flowers gossip, a secret to bestow.

Sun shines brightly, hats fly in the air,
Kids chase the shadows, with nary a care.
A butterfly lands, and pauses to stare,
At the picnic table with the cake laid bare.

A sandcastle crumbles, a grand little throne,
Its builder, a prince, takes it all in his own.
Seagulls squawking, they steal all the crumbs,
The merriment rises, as laughter becomes.

In this quiet moment, mischief at play,
The lighthearted echoes guide us away.
In veils of delight, we spin and we twirl,
Crafting a magic, a whimsical whirl.

Whirlwinds of Soft Touch

Pillow fights spark from a mischievous glance,
Fluffy projectiles make laughter enhance.
A dog in pajamas, oh what a sight,
Rolling and tumbling into the night.

Socks on the floor, a chaotic parade,
The fruit bowl chatting, their colors displayed.
A cake on the counter, say, with a frown,
Feels quite neglected; would prefer a crown.

In the kitchen, a pot-bellied chef,
Whispers to veggies, though wobbly and deaf.
With a pinch and a dash, they dance in the stew,
Creating a feast that's zany and new.

Bubbles invade at the end of the bath,
Creating a bubble, a slippery path.
With a splash and a giggle, the night grows late,
In whirlwinds of antics, we happily skate.

Shadows of the Uninvited

In the corner sits a sock without pair,
With stories to tell, but none seem to care.
Sneaky shadows leer, oh what a delight,
As they dance at the edges of flickering light.

A spoon holds a grudge, it clinks with a chill,
About the day it was left under the grill.
A fork and a knife plot, with all of their might,
To conquer the table and reclaim their right.

Footsteps echo in the hall with a thud,
As a mysterious cat stirs a great deal of mud.
With a flick of her tail, she winks at the night,
Leaving behind whispers, a curious fright.

In the corner, shadows shiver and sway,
As the uninvited join in on the play.
With giggles and hops, they silently clash,
Creating new legends in a whimsical flash.

Laces of Promise

In a world where knots misbehave,
Shoelaces dance like they're on a rave.
Chasing squirrels with a funny flair,
Unraveling dreams in the crisp air.

Slipping and tripping, oh what a sight,
Comedic tumbles, oh what a plight.
With each tangled mess, laughter unfolds,
As stories of mischief are daringly told.

Soft Desires in a Breeze

A feather floats by, what a tease,
It tickles your nose, oh how it frees.
Chasing it down leads to a fall,
Laughter erupts, you can't help but call.

The gentle sways in the summer light,
A dance of delight, a playful flight.
Whispers carry, oh so serene,
Yet laughter lurks in every scene.

The Fabric of Forgotten Tales

Once stitched with care and a hearty laugh,
The seams now frayed, a comical craft.
Old stories linger in the soft folds,
Revealing the joy that never grows old.

With patches of whimsy and threads of cheer,
They speak of adventures that we hold dear.
In the pockets of fabric, a treasure lies,
Where humor hides and nonsense flies.

Threads of a Quiet Lament

In silence, the stitches begin to weave,
A tale so funny, you'll hardly believe.
Misfortunes sewn with a twinkle of eye,
As giggles escape and worries run dry.

Quiet moments, yet bursts of delight,
Tangled yarns in the soft moonlight.
With every loop and twist, we find,
Laughter entwined with a playful mind.

Flickering Moments of Truth

In the corner, shadows dance,
A cat sneezed in a funny trance.
Colors swirl, then quickly fade,
Are those secrets or just charades?

Laughter bounces off the walls,
Cake crumbs fall during wild brawls.
Atop a chair, a squirrel spies,
Did it hear the latest lies?

Jelly beans and silly pranks,
A sideways glance at padded ranks.
In every giggle, truth does cling,
Wrapped tight in a joking ring.

So raise a glass to the absurd,
In moments fleeting, laughter's stirred.
The truth that wiggles, slips away,
In the joy of this kooky play.

Weaving Whispers in the Air

Balloons float with giggles near,
Invisible strings of joy and cheer.
An echo of secrets, soft and bright,
What did the cake say last night?

Wobbly tables and drinks that slosh,
A pie flung high—oh, what a nosh!
In the corner, a dance seems planned,
But who stepped on the ice cream stand?

Curious minds in a funny fray,
Spinning tales in the livelong day.
A hiccup here, a cackle there,
Friendship stitched with laughter's hair.

So gather round, let stories part,
In this crazy fun, we'll all take part.
Each whisper tickles like a dare,
A lively banter fills the air.

Silent Traces of Time

The clock ticks loud, a comical tease,
Its hands move slow, like a dancing breeze.
Chairs are stacked, each one a throne,
In a world where laughter has grown.

Life's fragrant cake, with layers and twists,
What's that lurking? Is it on the lists?
Jokes are made, and voices rise,
In this place where fun's the prize.

Bright balloons drift, soft as a sigh,
Chasing memories as they fly.
Whispers float in a playful way,
What else could happen on this silly day?

So off we go, with grins so wide,
In the echoes of cheer, let's abide.
Time may be silent, but not our bliss,
Let's laugh it off with a crazy kiss.

Unraveled Stories at Dusk

At dusk we find what's left untold,
Silly secrets, prize, and gold.
The pie's on the floor, a splatter surprise,
Whoever threw it? Oh, what a guise!

Footsteps shuffle, on the loose,
In this mystery, who's the juice?
A parrot laughs with flapping wings,
Surely it knew all the wild things.

Giggles burst, like popcorn pop,
Lost a sock? It must be a flop!
In tangled tales, we twist and spin,
Dusk becomes our playful kin.

So grab a snack and take a seat,
We'll unravel tales, oh so sweet.
In the midst of chaos, smiles glint,
This merry band knows how to print.

Silken Secrets in the Breeze

A flutter of fabric, oh what a sight,
Wiggling and jumping, it brings delight.
A cheeky gust tickles, like a playful tease,
Leaves me laughing under the dancing trees.

A giggle escapes from a nearby chair,
The curtains sway gently without a care.
Invisible friends in a swirling parade,
With whispers of mischief, they're never afraid.

The sun winks shyly, gold in its glow,
As tales of the fabric begin to flow.
Each drape and flirt, a wink of a prize,
Mirth in the air, in their playful guise.

Laughter erupts in the soft afternoon,
As fabric frolics to a merry tune.
Oh, what a jolly breeze comes to play,
With secrets and smiles to brighten the day.

Colors of an Unseen Presence

Dashes of color parade through the air,
Bright and bewildering, they dance without care.
They hide behind corners, giggling along,
Crafting a chorus, oh, what a song!

Rainbow-hued shadows, they tease and they prance,
Twisting and turning in a whimsical dance.
Do you feel them lurking, just out of reach?
Tickling the senses, oh, what a speech!

Sassy and sprightly, they swirl and they spin,
A riot of hues, where does one begin?
Colors revolt with joy, can't help but jest,
Chasing each other, they're never at rest.

In every small corner, they frolic and peek,
Sending you giggles—come take a sneak.
With light-hearted revelry and laughter for free,
A carnival painted in joyful decree.

Murmured Patterns of the Night

Under the moon's glow, a soft giggle flows,
Patterns emerge where the cool wind blows.
A patchwork of laughter is stitched in the dark,
Tiny quirks quilted where mischief can spark.

Crickets join in with their chirpy refrain,
A symphony woven with whispers of grain.
The shadows hold stories, each tale so spry,
Entangled in glee, they dance in the sky.

Muffled chuckles echo in the still air,
As laughter and patterns twist everywhere.
The night wears a cloak of mirth and delight,
Where stories abound and the fun takes flight.

As oak trees sway in a gentle embrace,
You'll find hidden grins on each furry face.
Let's tiptoe through starlight, so snug and polite,
In the quiet of darkness, such joy ignites.

The Soft Lilt of Hidden Stories

In corners of rooms, soft tales start to climb,
Whispering secrets, they dance out of rhyme.
A giggle from behind, a flutter, a tease,
The stories unfold with such playful ease.

Tiny voices chuckle under the bed,
With tales of adventures, they're easily fed.
Each cushion narrates a tale of delight,
Where shadows become friends in the pale light.

The clock on the wall nods in agreement,
As plush toys gossip, planning their ascent.
With every soft creak, a giggly delight,
A saga of laughter blooms into the night.

In the cozy of whispers, the fun intertwines,
With laughter and antics forming the lines.
Soon every heart beats in joyous repose,
In a world full of stories, where joy simply flows.

Subtle Ties of Longing

In the corner, a knotted string,
Giggles erupt as it starts to swing.
A dance of colors, twirls in the air,
Chasing each other without a care.

Each pull a reminder of unspoken charms,
Tickling hearts, it plays with alarms.
A tug here, a yank there, oh what a sight,
As laughter erupts, we twirl through the night.

Patterns emerge in a playful spree,
No need for plans, just you and me.
Around and around, like a merry-go-round,
In this tangled web, pure joy is found.

At the end of the day when the laughter fades,
We'll reminisce about our funny escapades.
With a wink and a nudge, we'll unravel this thread,
In the game of connections, we've danced instead.

Silken Secrets Entwined

A whisper of lace on a sunny day,
Bumbling bees buzzing in their own play.
Caught on a breeze, a giggle takes flight,
Chasing after secrets hidden from sight.

With each flicker, the air starts to glow,
Tangles and knots in a curious flow.
Tickling toes as we swish and we sway,
In this colorful chaos, we laugh all the way.

A flick of the wrist sends patterns afloat,
Lessons in friendship from a teetering boat.
Laughter is woven through each little snare,
As we tumble and roll, without a care.

With threads intertwined, our stories unfold,
For in silly moments, we become bold.
So here's to the dance, to the threads we embrace,
In the tapestry of joy, we find our place.

The Softness of Bare Intentions

Under the moon on a warm summer's night,
Barefoot adventures, oh what a sight!
Whispers of mischief, a flicker in time,
As we plot and we plan, oh so sublime.

A hop, skip, and jump, we're lightly undone,
Each moment a treasure, a race just for fun.
With a wink and a grin, we dance in our dream,
Life's sweet little secrets, unraveling seam.

Around and around, confusion takes hold,
Like a riddle unraveled, the tale is retold.
Each soft little giggle, a spark in the air,
Together we stand, with goofy flair.

So let's not forget the lightness of heart,
In this playful chaos, each plays a part.
With bare intentions and laughter that sways,
We find our delight in the silliest ways.

Chasing Shadows with Delicate Fingers

In the twilight glow, with fingers so light,
We reach for the shadows that dance in the night.
A game of illusions, the laughter ignites,
As we chase the phantoms of soft little flights.

Each flick of the wrist brings giggles galore,
A tickle, a poke, we're always wanting more.
With delicate touches, we pirouette round,
In our world of silliness, joy does abound.

Like whispers of petals that float in the air,
The pranks that we pull are devil-may-care.
Who knew that shadows could be so much fun?
With a stumble and fall, we run till we're done.

So here's to the moments with laughter we share,
Chasing those shadows, without a care.
With delicate fingers and grins ear to ear,
In this light-hearted dance, there's nothing to fear.

The Veiled Connection of Two Souls

In a corner, they giggle, quite unseen,
Hiding secrets like a squirrel's stash of beans.
Their laughter dances through the air so bright,
Two minds entangled, lost in sheer delight.

A nod here, a wink there, the game is on,
Banter flows freely, a smile like a con.
With playful jabs and teasing in their gaze,
Each word a thread in a humorous maze.

In their world of twirls, they spin and sway,
Crafting joy in the most comical way.
Under a veil of mirth, they don't see,
How their whimsy twists into sheer glee.

Together they weave a tapestry bright,
Each stitch a joke, every patch feels right.
In this playful dance, a bond they create,
A connection so strong, it's truly first-rate.

A Chorus of Tangled Threads

In a room full of colors, they giggle and twine,
Jokes flying like confetti, oh how they shine!
With laughter like music, each note is a tease,
Unraveling joy like an expert with ease.

Twists in their stories create quite a mess,
But the humor entwined is anyone's guess.
A tug on a string sends a chuckle your way,
As friends craft a saga of whimsy at play.

With every snicker their friendship inflates,
Creating a harmony, joyous and great.
Mismatched sentiments fuse in one knot,
Each snip of the thread spins a tale that's hot.

Dancing through moments, they frolic and glide,
Together in laughter, they cannot hide.
In this chorus of joy, they'll always connect,
Finding delight in each little defect.

Fluid Conversations of the Heart

With a coffee cup perched on the edge of fate,
They swap silly stories, there's no need to wait.
Every word a splash, like laughter in streams,
In this banter-filled whirlpool, they follow their dreams.

Twirling about in a whirl of delight,
Every glance shared feels playful and light.
The words dance all over, a saucy ballet,
With winks and sly smiles leading the way.

Like rivers that flow without aim or control,
Conversations meander, keeping them whole.
In each silly tale, their hearts find a glow,
A puddle of joy where giggles can flow.

With every chuckle, their spirits take flight,
In fluid exchanges, their bonds ignite bright.
For in this fire, hilarity blooms,
Crafting moments that lighten dark rooms.

The Intricacies of Luminescent Knots

Tangled and twisted, their humor still shines,
In the chaos of laughter, where friendship aligns.
Each joke is a teetering rope of delight,
A measure of brightness that sparkles at night.

With knots made of giggles and ribbons of cheer,
They find joy in messing, holding friends near.
The trick is in laughter, no need for a plan,
Just a flick of a smile and a wink from the man.

Beneath the bright layers, a tale's waiting there,
Of blunders and mishaps, the charm in the air.
Each twist in their stories adds depth to their art,
Crafting a bond that won't ever depart.

A tapestry woven with threads that disclose,
That life's not so serious, as humor bestows.
In the world of the knotted, they find their release,
In laughter, they savor a little sweet peace.

The Sound of Shimmering Threads

In a cupboard, a secret is spun,
A thread of laughter, just for fun.
Socks in corners quietly sway,
Whispering tales of their holiday.

A needle pricks at the fabric grin,
Stitching up tales where the mischief's been.
Buttons jump in a jig with glee,
As scissors snip through the fabric free.

The Soft Armor of Invisibility

A cape unseen, I wear it proud,
Hiding beneath a busy crowd.
Oh, the mishaps that I ignite,
As I trip on shoes, out of sight!

An artful dodge, avoiding the mess,
In silence, I wear my silliness.
Invisible capers, cheeky and bright,
Who knew chaos could be such a delight?

Ethereal Echoes in the Weft

Fabrics whisper, strands intertwine,
Crafting giggles in every line.
A patchwork quilt, a story told,
Of socks once lost, now brave and bold.

Twinkling yarn, a cotton ball,
Rolling in corners, about to sprawl.
Laughter threads through each silly seam,
In the tapestry of a dreamer's dream.

The Dance of Fragile Memory

Memories twirl on the fabric's edge,
Seams of humor, a promise, a pledge.
Each stitch a giggle, each knot a grin,
Dancing along with the chaos within.

A fabric of thoughts, frayed at times,
But woven with jokes, and funny rhymes.
Oh, how we remember, with a chuckle or two,
The silly moments, in stitches we grew.

Ethereal Parleys of Softness

In a world where fluff resides,
Fuzzy critters dance with pride.
Tickled feathers fly about,
As giggles roam and chase the shroud.

Laughter echoes, oh so sweet,
Crafty paws with nimble feet.
A patchwork quilt of silly dreams,
Under starlight, every gleam.

Chirps and chuckles blend the night,
Whispers float, a soft delight.
Jovial nudges in the dark,
Creating sparks with every spark.

From shadows leap the cheeky sprites,
Playful jests in fleeting flights.
With glimmers bright, the soft parade,
Sowed in joy, a frolic made.

Threads of Companionship

Beneath the stitches of our fate,
Laughter binds, it's never late.
Two hearts woven, tales unfold,
In lively yarns and colors bold.

Each knot a memory, bright and clear,
Every pull, a note of cheer.
With humor sew a twinkling patch,
Together, none can find the catch.

We roll the fabric of our days,
In playful patterns and funny ways.
Like misfit socks who dare to dance,
Life's silliness, a sweet romance.

So thread me close, with zany ties,
In friendship's warmth, our laughter flies.
A tapestry of jests and grins,
Stitched together through thick and thin.

Murmurs of a Gentle Breeze

In breezes soft, the whispers play,
Like tickled leaves in light ballet.
They tease the cats, who swat in vain,
As chuckles float like summer rain.

Around the trees, in gentle sways,
Swaying branches join the craze.
Chirpy banter, oh so light,
Brings grins to faces, pure delight.

Puffing clouds in cotton fluff,
Giggling winds just can't get enough.
Each gust a note in nature's song,
Together we find where we belong.

With breezy jests, we'll twirl and spin,
In whispered laughs, let the fun begin.
As joy evolves in airy themes,
We chase the sun's soft, playful beams.

Hints of Past Emotions

In corners dim, where echoes creep,
Lurk moments soft, memories heap.
Silly smiles from days gone by,
A wink, a nod, a wistful sigh.

Through tangled tales of joy and cheer,
We find the threads of laughter here.
With gentle nudges, we recall,
The pratfalls shared, the rise, the fall.

Giggling ghosts of yesteryears,
Bring giggles forth, as time adheres.
Hints of mischief in old chats,
Remind us all of silly spats.

So let us raise a cup to then,
And share the spice of what has been.
With past's rib-tickling embrace,
We twirl in joy, a timeless grace.

A Symphony in Silent Strands

In the corner, a cat pranced,
While the dog just stared, entranced.
Tangled threads in a goofy dance,
Creating chaos with every chance.

A broomstick's hat flew past my head,
Turning the room where mischief spread.
The vacuum roared like a beast unsaid,
As socks slipped off, the laundry fled.

Laughter erupted in every room,
As hats took flight and brooms found gloom.
The dog, now chasing a paper plume,
Declared it royalty, all in bloom.

In this ballet of furry delight,
We found our footing, laughing bright.
For every twist and turn at night,
Brought us joy, a silly sight.

Dreamy Touches and Hidden Hues

Bright colors spilled on the floor today,
In a world where shades want to play.
Pinks and greens in a grand array,
Making the walls want to sway.

A paintbrush slipped, oh what a mess,
Creating chaos, we must confess.
With giggles erupting, we can just guess,
That art's not perfect, it's pure excess.

The cat dipped a paw in blue delight,
And strolled across canvas, what a sight!
Tickled by laughter that took flight,
We painted the day into the night.

When colors danced to their own sweet tune,
In a riot of hues, under the moon.
Every drop a joke, a light-hearted boon,
As we captured giggles, and fun was strewn.

The Sway of Hidden Stories

In the attic where dust bunnies thrive,
Old tales awaken, come alive.
Boxes bursting with secrets contrive,
A hat on a mannequin, oh what a dive!

A pair of shoes with a dance of their own,
Frog jumps and twirls, never alone.
They clicked and clacked on a wooden throne,
Making memories from stories unknown.

The clock chimed loudly, what a surprise,
As products of past raised their eyes.
They reminisced of whimsical ties,
Sharing laughter beneath old skies.

With each dusty trunk, a new charade,
On paths where memories softly wade.
In awkward twirls, the stories played,
In colors of joy, we all remontade.

Ethereal Layers of Sound

In the kitchen pots sang a tune,
With spoons drumming like a lively rune.
Chickens clucked, a raucous balloon,
As music of laughter filled the room.

The kettle whistled a silly song,
While dancing around, we all joined along.
The blender whirred, trying to be strong,
To drown our giggles, but how could it be wrong?

Mismatched socks tapped to the beat,
As echoes of joy bounced off our feet.
With each little sound, life felt complete,
In the rhythm of chaos, we found our seat.

At the end of the day, all gathered around,
The fruits of laughter universally found.
In the symphony of play, joy profound,
We danced to the melody, forever unbound.

Hems of Longing

In a closet, secrets hide,
A sock with dreams, oh what a ride!
Threads of hope, a knot so tight,
Stitching wishes in the night.

Button eyes and crooked seams,
Filling tailors' wacky dreams.
A hem that trips, a giggle shared,
Whirling fabric, oh how we dared!

Lost in folds, we laugh aloud,
Chasing laughter, lost in a crowd.
Curtains twirl, a dance begins,
Caught in fabric's playful spins.

Yet amidst the laughter's song,
Lies a fabric where we belong.
In stitches tight, adventures flow,
In every seam, funny tales grow.

Edges of Grace

A tutu spins with charming flair,
Poodle skirts twirl like they don't care.
Ruffles wobble, pirouettes glide,
Laughter echoes, joy won't hide.

Crooked collars on a blazer tight,
School days bright, oh what a sight!
Faded jeans with stories wear,
Silly moments dance in air.

A bowtie bows, with style quite rare,
Jokes on polka dots in the fair.
With every hem, a laugh spills out,
Dancing dreams, we twist about.

At the seams, adventure waits,
With little giggles, it creates.
Let's stitch some joy, weave the fun,
In fabric's embrace, we have won.

Enigmas in Frayed Edges

Curly threads tell tales so fine,
Braided fibres laugh like wine.
With every snag, a secret spools,
Stitching giggles, breaking rules.

Frayed edges, oh what a sight,
Worn-out jeans feel just right.
Pockets bulge with silly things,
Spare change, dreams, and joyful flings.

Mystery grows in seams undone,
Each tug suggests we've had some fun.
Patterns clash like weekend plans,
Twists and turns in ditching bands.

Beware the hem that comes to play,
It trips us up in a funny way.
In every snip and possibly tear,
Lies a quirk, free as air.

The Lure of Untold Stories

Beneath the lace, a tale does hide,
Unraveled secrets, untamed pride.
Every stitch a secret tale,
Giggles echo, laughter prevail.

Stitched away in woven bliss,
A clumsy patch, oh what a miss!
Each fabric fold, a laugh ensued,
Tales unfold, and moods renewed.

Faded patterns, life unfolds,
Every snip, a joke retold.
With quirky tales in fray and fold,
These silly threads are worth their gold.

Whispers lost in woven dreams,
Beneath the fabric, laughter beams.
In every seam, bright stories lie,
Waiting for the bold to try.

Echoes beneath the Fabric

Echoes laugh in garments bright,
Twists and turns, a pure delight.
A croaky hem, a giggle near,
Fabric sings when friends are here.

In the pockets, whispers play,
Crazy socks want to ballet.
Jokes unfold in wrinkles there,
Woven secrets, quirkiness bare.

Tails of jackets swirl and tease,
With every loop, we catch the breeze.
Ribbons twist with flair and fun,
As laughter weaves, we two become one.

Beneath the layers, stories bloom,
With every fold, we chase the gloom.
In the dance of fabric, we find the grace,
Together, everywhere, we embrace.

Fluttering Hues of Unspoken Dreams

Colors dance in wild delight,
They twirl around, a silly sight.
A canvas spills with giggles bright,
As rainbows chase the day to night.

Pinks and greens play leapfrog too,
A playful cat, a curious shoe.
Caught in the breeze, a dream in lieu,
With laughter sprouting, who knew who?

Fleeting thoughts take wing and soar,
They bump and crash, then giggle more.
In the air, a joke does pour,
Life's silly tunes we can't ignore.

Under stars, we'll weave these schemes,
Chasing shadows of our dreams.
With every twist, laughter beams,
In a world that's as fun as it seems.

A Tapestry of Secrets

Threads so bright and secrets spun,
A kitten plays, and we all run.
Whispers hide in the morning sun,
As giggles twinkle, we have fun.

A needle's wink, a laughing thread,
What's left unsaid bounces instead.
In this fabric, humor's spread,
Where every tale's a playful dread.

Colors clash in joyful mess,
What lies beneath? Just a guess.
We'll stitch together happiness,
In patterns bold, anxiety less.

Laughter weaves through every seam,
As we unravel silly dreams.
In tangled threads, our friendship beams,
Creating joy from whims and schemes.

Gentle Murmurs in Twilight

In the dusk, soft giggles fall,
A breeze sings low, teasing us all.
Leaves rustle like a friendly call,
As shadows play on the garden wall.

Silly stories twist and twirl,
With whispers shared in a playful whirl.
Dusk's canvas starts to unfurl,
As laughter spirals and diamonds pearl.

Beware the crickets on the prowl,
They've got jokes that make you howl.
In twilight's glow, watch them scowl,
As we munch on treats and sing 'till a growl.

Each soft murmur hides a jest,
In winding paths, we seek the best.
With every hush, our hearts feel blessed,
As night descends, we play and rest.

The Rhythm of Woven Dreams

In stitches bright, our dreams collide,
With clumsy steps, we twist and glide.
A rhythm beats, a joyful ride,
As laughter's thread takes us inside.

Funky patterns and silly shapes,
With giggles bouncing like silly tapes.
Every mishap, a tale that scrapes,
In the fabric, the fun reshapes.

A whirl of colors, splashes loud,
As we twirl and swirl, feeling proud.
With every laugh, we form a crowd,
In this dance of dreams, we're endowed.

Let's gather 'round and share a cheer,
For woven dreams, our hearts hold dear.
With every stitch, we'll persevere,
In this rhythm, let's laugh and steer.

The Traveling Echo of Overlapping Threads

A stitch came loose, oh what a sight,
The cat wore it as a hat, quite a fright.
Grandma laughed, a snort and a cheer,
As threads danced round, spreading good cheer.

The dog joined in, tail wagging so fast,
Chasing those scraps, the fun unsurpassed.
Each tug and pull, a game of delight,
Creating a mess, yet hearts felt so light.

Necklaces made from lengths of old twine,
Fashion for pets, a runway divine.
With mismatched designs, they strutted so bold,
A fashion week tale worth telling when old.

So wave goodbye to comfort and neat,
In chaos and laughter, our lives feel complete.
With threads intertwined, we'll wander and tread,
Creating the tales wherein laughter is spread.

Echoes of a Weaving Heart

In a loom of giggles, we crafted our dreams,
Each thread a chuckle, as wild as it seems.
Fingers danced with yarn, oh what a show,
Weaving the nonsense, we let our hearts flow.

A butterfly landed, all covered in fluff,
It twirled in the air, just to get tough.
The neighbors peered out, some frowned and some smiled,
At the sight of our antics, they laughed like a child.

With humor entwined, we made quite a scene,
Creating odd patterns, and costumes unseen.
Who knew that the mishaps could spark so much fun,
As we spun tales woven, together as one.

So here's to the threads that tangle and twist,
For in the chaos, pure bliss can't be missed.
With hearts intertwined, let the laughter abound,
In this fabric of joy, our happiness found.

Fleeting Hints in the Twilight

In the dusk, where shadows play light tag,
A bemused frog wore a bright yellow rag.
He croaked out a tune, not a care in the world,\nAs
fireflies twinkled and nearby folks twirled.

An owl hooted once, then started to sway,
While singing a song that led night into day.
Bats flapped around in a comical dance,
The air filled with giggles, who'd miss such a chance?

We gathered our friends for a festival cheer,
With laughter that echoed for everyone near.
A bonfire glowing, flickering bright,
As stories were shared, fueling the night.

In the twilight's embrace, with a wink and a grin,
The night brought together all the quirks within.
For hints of delight drifted wide in the air,
In fleeting moments, we found joy to share.

The Subtle Opulence of Untold Stories

In a garden of tales, where the daisies all wink,
Lived characters strange who adored a good drink.
A gnome with a pipe blew bubbles of tea,
While the cat offered sips, 'Come join, just be free!'

A turtle, quite tipsy, sang songs from a shell,
With tunes of his youth that he sang oh so well.
The moon giggled softly, the stars winked in tune,
As mischief unfolded beneath the bright moon.

Petunias planned dances with marigold friends,
While the daisies giggled at all that transcends.
Each story a stitch in the fabric of night,
Creating a tapestry woven in light.

So here's to the moments that twindle and twist,
In the dance of the quirky, who knows what you'll miss?
In gardens of laughter, let humor reclaim,
The beauty of life, wild, crazy, no shame.

The Dance of Delicate Threads

In the corner, a cat takes a leap,
Chasing shadows that wiggle and creep.
The yarn starts to sway, oh what a tease,
Like a dance party thrown by the breeze.

Spools roll around, like they're on a spree,
Knitting needles tap, a wild jubilee.
Laughter erupts, as stitches unwind,
A riot of color, hilarity combined.

Crafty little hands, all tangled with glee,
Who knew crafting could be so carefree?
With each playful tug, and each playful twist,
The fabric of friendship can't be missed!

So here's to the threads, and their comical play,
They lift our spirits in the silliest way.
In every tight knot, a giggle we find,
As we dance with delight, let our fancies unwind.

Secrets Tied in Knots

In the attic, a treasure we seek,
Fuzzy old socks, and a shoe with a squeak.
A knot in the laces, a riddle to solve,
As we giggle and play, the chaos evolves.

Behind the cupboard, a mystery brews,
A spaghetti of strings, in vibrant hues.
The cats plot a heist, oh what a sight,
While we try to manage this colorful flight.

A hat with no head, yet wearing a grin,
Winks at the crowd, oh what a din!
Each tangle we giggle, each loop we adore,
In the secrets we find, we always want more.

So let's tie a new knot, with laughter and cheer,
In each inventive twist, our joys will endear.
With bright bits of yarn and squeaky delight,
We unravel the humor, from day into night.

Echoes of the Unseen

A bump in the night, what could it be?
An unseen mischief, tickling with glee.
A ghost made of fluff, with a glimmering grin,
Whirls in the dark, let the fun begin!

Through curtains that flutter, we hear the faint sound,
Of giggles and chuckles that float all around.
A sock on the floor pulls a prank on the cat,
As the kittens embark on a romping attack.

Unraveling stories from corners we know,
Where shadows and humor put on quite a show.
With each twist and turn, a chuckle or two,
In the echoes of night, our dreams come true.

So let's raise our glasses, to the follies unseen,
To playfulness hidden, yet bursting like cream.
In the depths of the dark, our laughter will soar,
While whispers of joy dance just outside the door.

Hushed Adornments of Night

At dusk, the world dons a silken robe,
Stars twinkle like gems in a cosmic globe.
The moon stifles laughter, a cheeky old chap,
As shadows come out for a playful lap.

Whispers of breezes, secrets afloat,
An owl on a mission, wears a small coat.
With every soft rustle, it seems to conspire,
To tickle the night, with its mischievous choir.

A squirrel in pajamas, quite proud of its flair,
Is zooming through branches without a care.
The laughter of crickets creates quite the tune,
As we gather the night in our glittering boon.

So here's to adventures beneath the moonlight,
Celebrating our quirks in the magical night.
May the stars hear our glee, as we spin and we dance,
With hushed adornments that lead us to chance!

Threads of Chance

In laughter's weave, a stitch gone awry,
Buttons pop off as we both laugh and cry.
The cat pranced in, with a sudden attack,
Now there's more yarn on the floor than on track.

A thread unspools, a dance in the air,
We trip and tumble, without a care.
Knots form and twist, like old stories told,
With giggles and snorts, our joys unfold.

Chasing our tails like a playful game,
Every twist and turn is never the same.
The spinning of fate, oh what a sight,
In the chaos, we find our delight.

So here's to the tangles and all of their charm,
Each twist and turn keeps us safe from harm.
Laughter like thread, it binds us so tight,
In the fabric of life, we dance through the night.

The Veil of Indistinct Paths

A curious road with signs all askew,
'Go left!' it proclaims, then bids you adieu.
We wander a forest where shadows confer,
Finding the way with a chuckle and purr.

Behind every bush lies a tale most absurd,
Where squirrels play cards and trees sing a word.
In circles we tread, like a loop on repeat,
Lost in giggles, we shuffle our feet.

A path lined with snacks, oh what a delight,
We munch on the treats till we're full, what a sight!
Confused by the map and the signs that mislead,
Turning in circles, we follow our greed.

Our journey is silly, with joy as our guide,
In this maze of nonsense, we take it in stride.
For every wrong turn is a laugh in the making,
In the veil of confusion, our hearts keep on baking.

Gentle Urgencies in Layered Tales

A cat in a hat with a timepiece so grand,
Rushed off to the party, with cake in his hand.
His tail curled in panic, oh what a sight,
The cake never made it, but laughter took flight.

A frog with a tune leaps into the fray,
The notes turn to giggles, they frolic and sway.
In stories so layered, the truth hides away,
As whimsy unfolds in its charming display.

We chase after minutes, they tick-tock and tease,
With mishaps aplenty that bring us to knees.
But sighs turn to chuckles, the best kind of race,
Wrapped up in our tales, we find joy in the chase.

So raise up a cup to the whims and the waits,
In layer upon layer, our laughter creates.
For each gentle urgency hides a grand tale,
Where fun waits around every twist of the trail.

Robust Echoes from Soft Corners

In corners so soft, where pillows conspire,
Echoes of giggles soar higher and higher.
A dragon made of fluff, oh what a sight,
Waging soft battles that echo with light.

With every small bicker, a laugh erupts loud,
Who knew that fun could gather a crowd?
The shadows hold secrets of games we once played,
In echoes that linger, our memories stayed.

A tickle here, and a poke over there,
Like whispers of mischief that float in the air.
In cozy absurdity, this is our stage,
Where silliness dances, and humor is sage.

So lean into laughter, let it be known,
In soft corners wrapped, we're never alone.
For robust echoes of joy will remain,
In each little nook where we play once again.

Fringes of Comfort and Unease

In a world of threads so bright,
Hats and scarves take to flight.
Some get tangled, others bliss,
Fashion's dance, we hardly miss.

Puppies chew on yarns so fine,
While kittens plot their grand design.
Laughter echoes in the room,
As needles click and stitch take zoom!

Unexpected knots arise,
As we tie up our own lies.
A frayed edge here, a loop there,
And we wobble in our flair.

But in this tapestry we weave,
Funny tales, we can't believe!
Life's a quilt of silly plays,
Gap stitched laughter fills our days.

The Harmony of Knotted Stories

Once a tale started to tangle,
With fairy dust and a jolly jangle.
Every twist, a laugh may bring,
In this dance, we're all the king.

Threads of humor run so free,
Like runaway cats up a tree.
We'll share our yarn with glee tonight,
As dreams say, 'Yes, that's just right!'

Knots tight like the jokes we spin,
Pull one loose, and let the fun begin.
The loom's a stage for our delight,
Each stitch a reason to ignite.

So gather round for tales of cheer,
Where laughter's thread entwined is near.
Swaps of yarn and playful wit,
Create a world that's truly hit.

The Veiled Speech of the Loom

The loom spins secrets in disguise,
Whispers of joy that rise and rise.
Colors clash in a bright array,
Where patterns decide to have their say.

Fabric talks, and oh, what a hoot,
With sassy threads and dancing boots.
A startled kitten jumps so high,
While bobbins laugh as they go by.

From tangled tales to threadbare dreams,
Life's a quilt of oddball schemes.
Stitches sing a hilarious tune,
Under the light of the silly moon.

So let's pull that yarn with flair,
And weave our laughter everywhere.
In this tapestry, let's play along,
Crafting joy, our favorite song.

Ensnared in Pliant Murmurs

In the web of loops and twirls,
Pet cats watch, with curious swirls.
We make up names for every hue,
In this playful painter's view.

The laughs bubble up like fresh whipped cream,
As threads twist and dance in a dream.
Caught in issues that seem so dire,
But humor makes everything higher.

A scarf that strangles, a sock that flies,
In our world of clumsy ties.
Each error is a treat to share,
As yarns unite, without a care.

So join the fun, don't be shy,
Let humor be the reason why.
In this fabric of light and fate,
We stitch together, we celebrate!

Hidden Ties to the Moonlit Night

Under the glow of shining beams,
Cats dance while chasing dreams.
Giggling leaves swirl and twirl,
As crickets play their nightly whirls.

Bouncing lightly, stars lose their hats,
While owls hoot and tell their chats.
The breeze whispers tales so fleet,
As frogs croak a goofy beat.

A raccoon wearing a paper crown,
Filters through the evening gown.
The moon chuckles, a jolly sight,
A party that lasts all through the night.

So join the fun beneath the glow,
Where giggles and shadows steal the show.
In this waltz of the cosmos bright,
We dance with joy, till dawn's first light.

Memories Adorned with Purpose

A hat made of breadcrumbs and chime,
Reminds a squirrel it's party time.
With doughnuts hanging from a tree,
The raccoon nods, 'This is the key!'

Old birds chat of grand old days,
Where worms danced in sunny rays.
Their tales spin in delightful loops,
As the world giggles at feathery scoops.

Mice don sneakers tiny and bright,
Preparing to race in the moon's soft light.
Their laughter echoes, a playful cheer,
While sleepy flowers yawn and peek near.

Beneath the stars, the stories swirl,
In a twinkling, silly, glittering whirl.
Memories woven in whimsical spree,
Nature's antics invite us to be free.

Whispered Textures of the Night Sky

Stars wear pajamas made of light,
As frogs fashion hats in delight.
The moon serves lemonade from afar,
While fireflies twinkle like a movie star.

Breezes tell secrets, soft and sly,
Of trees shaking leaves that nearby lie.
Each fluttering leaf, a giggling sigh,
As shadows act out a playful why.

Bunnies hop in a conga line,
With tiny shoes that glitter and shine.
They dance under the glimmer's bright blare,
As beetles roll marbles without a care.

Past midnight, the antics ignite,
With laughter echoing into the night.
The universe pulses, a jubilant scheme,
As all join in the frolicsome dream.

The Tapestry of Soft Secrets

A blanket of giggles we weave just so,
Where butterflies gossip while putting on a show.
Frolicking breezes tickle the tall grass,
While globes of starlight in unison pass.

Old toads sporting tiny neckties bright,
Trade jokes and riddles in the fading light.
The crickets chuckle, composing in tune,
As the fireflies choreograph a dance to the moon.

With whispers woven into each stitch,
Even the shadows can dance and hitch.
The joy of the night, like a playful tease,
Wraps all in the warmth of a zany breeze.

So tiptoe softly through laughter and play,
In this world where silliness finds its way.
A tapestry of chuckles, bright and spry,
Shares secrets of fun beneath the sky.

www.ingramcontent.com/pod-product-compliance
Lightning Source LLC
Chambersburg PA
CBHW060109230426
43661CB00003B/129